Samuel Charters

A Sermon on Intercession and an Instruction Concerning Oaths

Second Edition

Samuel Charters

A Sermon on Intercession and an Instruction Concerning Oaths
Second Edition

ISBN/EAN: 9783337289997

Printed in Europe, USA, Canada, Australia, Japan

Cover: Foto ©Lupo / pixelio.de

More available books at **www.hansebooks.com**

A

SERMON

ON

INTERCESSION,

AND AN

INSTRUCTION

CONCERNING

OATHS.

By SAMUEL CHARTERS,

MINISTER OF WILTON.

THE SECOND EDITION,

HAWICK:

PRINTED BY GEORGE CAW,

M.DCC.LXXXV.

ADVERTISEMENT.

THE following SERMON was publifhed by the Society for propagating Chriftian Knowledge in 1779. AN INSTRUCTION CONCERNING OATHS was publifhed by the Prefbytery of Jedburgh in 1782. The alterations in this edition are made by the Author.

A

S E R M O N.

———⋅———

I TIMOTHY, ii. I.

INTERCESSIONS.

INTERCESSIONS have an effect on focial virtue.

PRAYER for our Country is a mean of loving it. The Pfalmift concludes his prayer for Jerufalem with this refolution, " I " will feek thy good." Love to the Public, when exalted by Prayer, difcovers itfelf in generous fentiment and heroic virtue. The voice of intereft, of pleafure, and of

A   every

every felfish paffion is put to filence. The
Lover of Truth and of his Country is ready,
in their caufe, to facrifice whatever is de-
fireable and dear. " Forgive their fin," faid
Mofes, when interceding for Ifrael, " for-
" give their fin I pray thee, or blot me out
" of the book which thou haft written." Ef-
her, when her people were devoted, con-
fecrated three days to Prayer, " after
" which I will go in unto the king which
" is not according to the Law, and if I
" perifh I perifh." Judas Maccabeus, in
the day of national calamity, retained in
the wildernefs, and cherifhed by Prayer,
love to his country and reverence for her
laws: his example animated a few friends:
by repeated fucceffes they greatly multi-
plied : " fighting with their hands and
" praying unto God with their hearts, they
" waxed valiant, out of weaknefs were
" made ftrong, and turned to flight the
" armies of the aliens."

WHILE war and rumours of war prevail, a relation to the Public, concern for
its interefts, and compaffion for human mifery

fery are deeply felt. Thefe feelings are expreffed in interceffion and fupplication. We contemplate the Almighty in his righteous judgments, correcting a luxurious felfifh fpirit, humbling the pride of wealth rank and dominion, calling forth the active and generous and fympathifing virtues. By faith we fee the cloud diffolve. " Sure-" ly the wrath of man fhall praife thee."

ABRAHAM's interceffion for Sodom did not avert the impending judgment; but he felt a generous concern for human nature, he enjoyed communion with God, and entered into the plan of his providence in fhewing favour to the wicked for the fake of the righteous. Inftead of a carelefs indifference and cold infenfibility, he looked toward Sodom, pondering the ways of God. " I will fing of judgment and of " mercy: to thee, O Lord, will I fing."

THE CHURCH OF CHRIST is an object more liberal and extenfive than our native land, and attracts more powerfully the prayers of Chriftians. " Thy kingdom

A 2   come.

" come. Thy will be done on earth as it
" is in heaven." We feel ourfelves the
fubjects of a kingdom not of this world,
and every child of God our fellow-citizen.
We feel an union of fpiritual interefts, and
privileges, and hopes. Zeal paffes from
the brighteft temporal object; and fixes
on righteoufnefs, peace, and joy in the Ho-
ly Ghoft.

In praying for the Church, it is of confequence to know for what we pray. Public fpirit, when mifguided, violates the
laws; and a mifguided zeal for the Church
of Chrift violates his law of love. The
church of Chrift is not limited by any
particular form of worfhip, or government,
or belief; it comprehends all who love the
Lord Jefus in fincerity. Our external conftitution, like the fabric in which we worfhip, will fall into decay, and the form will
be changed; but the reign of Chrift is in
the hearts of men. " So long as the fun
" and moon endure, a Seed fhall ferve
" him."

WHILE

WHILE devout love extends to Chriſtians of every denomination, we contemplate
the hand of Providence in the different
ways of thinking among men. Theſe call
forth the exerciſe of reaſon, and lead to
the diſcovery of truth. They kindle a zeal
for truth which made Paul aſſert and vin-
dicate, in oppoſition to Peter, the liberty
wherewith Chriſt has made us free. From
the days of Paul many able aſſertors of liberty have ariſen. Tyranny over the human underſtanding has been reſiſted even
unto blood; and, after the ſtruggle of ages,
the air of liberty is breathed again. We
behold abounding ſects, as ſo many pledges
of the right of private judgment——a ſacred
right, which it is the glory of this nation
and of this age to reſpect.

THERE is indeed a dark ſide. Strife
and contention ſometimes mingle. This
is a memorial of human frailty. Deſire
ſprings forward to the reſt that remains.
We look up to God " who ſtills the noiſe
" of the waves and the tumults of the
" people," and trace the operation of his
Providence.

Providence. Divifions, which were formed in anger and ftained with blood, redound
to the increafe of knowledge and forbear-
ance. Principle is refpected, and miftakes
are pardoned. The multitude of fects a-
bates their animofity. They are drawn together again by the band of love, and at
laft conclude, That " to fear God and keep
" his commandments is the whole of
" man."

IN praying for all men, we remember
that they are brethren ; that we fhall fleep
together in the duft ; that we are fellow-
travellers to a land where ftrife and contention, anger and debate, pride and hypo-
crify fhall prevail no more. We join our
prayers and praifes with thofe who fear
God and work righteoufnefs, of every nation and kindred and language. " Let the
" people praife thee, O Lord, let all the
" people praife thee."

WHILE prayers for the public weal
are offered up, there is often, it muft be
owned, a liftlefs indifference in our affem-
blies.

blies. Whether it be that the object is too great, or that the famenefs tires, or that our method be defective, or that human laws accord not with the fpirit of prayer, or that love to the public and zeal for religion be indeed waxing cold; or whatever elfe be the caufe, the effect is vifible. I fhall therefore profecute the argument in particular and familiar inftances.

INTERCESSION improves and regulates parental love. Can a mother forget her fucking child, compaffed about with dangers by night and by day, the leaft of which may deftroy? Can fhe better exprefs her compaffion, and enfure the fuccefs and comfort of her own care and watchfulnefs, than by committing her child to "the Shepherd of Ifrael, who flumbers "not nor fleeps?"

YOUTH is the feafon of temptation. While Job's children were feafting, "he "offered burnt-offerings according to the "number of them all; for Job faid, It may "be my children have finned." Interceffion directs

directs parental love, not to the wealth and beauty and worldly honour ; but rather to the innocence and piety of children.

MANY of our young men go abroad, e-fpecially in war. To parents the hour of feparation is dark. They follow their children in devout affection through fcenes of manifold danger and temptation. Reft returns to their fouls in committing them to God, who is " the confidence of all the " ends of the earth, and of them that are " afar off upon the fea."

EVEN in the cafe of a degenerate child, hope is cherifhed by communion with him who " waiteth to be gracious."

THE affectionate fupplication of parents may prove a mean of reclaiming the prodigal. In a folitary hour he will perhaps reflect on their unmerited affection, and liften to the voice of nature, and meditate a return to virtue. Thefe reflections, it is true, are fwept away in the next excefs of riot. They will recur however and

and make a deep impreſſion, ſo ſoon as diſ-
eaſe or want or impriſonment has brought
him to himſelf. Beginning in good earneſt to relent, and to think if any mean of
reconciliation be yet in his power; he is
not a little encouraged by the devout concern of his parents. If they be earneſt to
obtain forgiveneſs from God, they them-
ſelves will not withhold forgiveneſs.

THE prayer which little children are
taught to put up for their father and their
mother, may be conſidered as the beginning
of piety and filial love, and a mean of un-
folding them.

OBJECTIONS have indeed been made
to the teaching of piety to children; and
a well known writer on education has con-
demned it †. In a queſtion of this kind,

parents

---

† ROUSSEAU ſeems to be an enemy to prayer in
every form. " I thank God for his gifts; but I do
" not pray to him. What ſhould I aſk?" He pro-
feſſes " not to philoſophize with his pupil, but to aſ-
" ſiſt him in conſulting his own heart." And is there

not

parents will judge for themfelves; but, in forming a judgment, they might enquire, If there be inftinctive regards to a heavenly as well as to earthly parents; if a tafte for

not in the heart a tendency to prayer, ftrongly felt at times; as in danger, which human power cannot a-vert; in perplexity, from which human prudence can-not extricate; under forrow, for which this world yields no confolation; and under the pangs of an a-wakened confcience? And is there not a fimilar ten-dency to interceffion? "God help you," is a common and natural exclamation when the help of man is vain. "The Lord have mercy on your foul," are the laft words when fentence of death is pronounced. It is the returning fentiment of compaffion which paffes from the feverity of juftice to a tribunal where mercy may be found. Why do the people defire the pray-ers of prophets and faints, and eftimate their prayers according to their fanctity? Was it not a dictate of the heart that made the mothers of Ifrael bring their little children to Jefus, that he might put his hands on them and pray? What means that ancient practice of afking a parent's bleffing, afking it in the moft in-terefting moments, when they leave their father's houfe, or when, on his death-bed, he bids them a laft farewell? And why does a parent's curfe in thofe in-terefting moments make the blood run cold? Rouffeau himfelf for Devotion, as well as for propriety and elegance, may improve by culture ; if early impreſſions of piety be apt to recur after youthful diſſipation had ſeemed to efface them ; and if they who do not remember their Creator in the days of their youth be likely ever to remember him. They might enquire what this meaneth, " Suffer " little children to come unto me ;" and what this promiſe meaneth, " They that " ſeek me early ſhall find me."

AFFECTION deſcends, and love to parents is not ſo eaſily retained as love to children. Moſt of the paſſions ſubſide with age, and the laſt human paſſion which warms the heart is love to children. The young are agitated with new connections and purſuits, which obſtruct the returns of

himſelf drops a philoſophy which accords ſo ill with human nature, and ſo very ill with the peculiar ſenſibility of his own heart; and deſcribes, in another part of his works, with his uſual eloquence, the tendency to interceſſion, with its conſoling and reclaiming power, in the caſe of a believing wife for an unbelieving huſband.

filial

filial love. Prayer for parents might, in some meafure, remove thofe obftructions. Even in foreign lands, and amidft bufy fcenes, the heart would melt at times with the remembrance of aged parents, and yield many foothing acknowledgements of the debt of love which they ftill owe.

THE prayers of parents with and for their children have an effect on filial love. "I blefs the Lord," fays Mr Flavel, "for "a religious tender father, who often "poured out his foul to God for me. This "ftock of prayers and bleffings I efteem "above the faireft inheritance on earth." With one who is apt to reflect and feel, the remembrance of many prayers, which pious parents offered up, is a touching re-membrance, and draws to virtue. "Shall I trouble their reft by departing from inno-cence? Shall I fruftrate the laft ftrong de-fire of their parting fpirits? Can I doubt that the favour of God extends to the chil-dren of his worfhippers? From the day that they forfook me, his favour hath com-paffed me about, it ftill encompaffeth me."

—In

—In this train of thought, ancient affection revives, the force of example is felt, and the fweetnefs of promife, and the power of prayer.

THE Prayers of Hufband and Wife for each other tend to ftrengthen and fweeten their union. Affection may decline, it may be interrupted by fallies of unguarded paffion, it may be foured by peevifhnefs. Thefe evils might be prevented by praying for each other. When they call to mind in the prefence of God, the relation by which they are connected, and the duties which belong to it, they feel an indifpenfible obligation to fulfil them. Every neglect is perceived to be wrong. Infidelity is thought of with horror, as a violation of the oath of God, and the utter extinction of domeftic peace. A fenfe of duty is brought in to the aid of affection by prayer ; nor is there a likelier method to revive affection, and re-eftablifh kind offices upon their true foundation.

If

If the yoke be unequal, prayer is a resource to the believer. A believing wife, who meets with unkindnefs where fhe looked for love, and had reafon to expect it, filently takes up her crofs, intercedes with him who can change the heart, and overcomes evil with good. The trial may be lengthened out, but prayer opens the defigns of Providence. Your way is hedged with thorns, but they are planted by a father's hand. He makes the ftaff of human comfort pierce through your hand and break under you, that his own rod and ftaff may comfort you. Great is the reward of meeknefs and patience, of prayers and tears, of humble filent defpifed virtue.

INTERCESSION fuftains and elevates Friendfhip. Prayer for an abfent friend revives ancient affection with a pleafing warmth. It unites us, as it were, in the prefence of that Being who fees at once the thoughts of every heart. We anticipate an everlafting union, and are animated in the way that leads to it.

IT

IT fupports and encourages a good man in the ways of goodnefs, to think that his friends intereft themfelves in the continuance and progrefs of his virtue, that they are inftant with God in his behalf.

IF he ever falls from innocence, he has this mournful confolation, that the friends of virtue weep with him ; that their fupplications afcend with his for pardon and reconciliation, for redoubled watchfulnefs and zeal; that the ftain on his chriftian profeffion may be wiped off, and the wound in his confcience healed.

SUPPLICATION for a brother overtaken in a fault conveys this caution to the fupplicant : " Let him that thinketh he ftand- " eth take heed left he fall."

THE prayers of a Minifter for the People to whom he minifters, lead to tendernefs and condefcenfion. They fubdue pride, impatience, and langour in the work of the miniftry. His foul is ftirred up with the elevating thought that he is a fellow-a fellow-worker together with God. Paul's prayer for the Ephefians is a pattern: " I " bow my knees to the Father of our Lord " Jefus Chrift, That he would grant you " according to the riches of his glory, " to be ftrengthened with might by his " Spirit in the inner man ; that Chrift " may dwell in your hearts by faith ; " that ye being rooted and grounded in " his love, may be able to comprehend " with all faints, what is the breadth, and " length, and depth, and height ; and " to know the love of Chrift, which paff- " eth knowledge, that ye might be fill- " ed with all the fulnefs of God." In the progrefs of this prayer the Apoftle warms, and glows, and labours for adequate language ; his own foul is filled with all that fulnefs. This is a natural effect of Interceffion. In the moments of communion with God, divine love is fhed abroad in the heart of the worfhipper, it is reflected on thofe who are dear to him, and expands in devout benevolence. To this exercife the Creator has annexed delight.

THE

THE delight indeed is tranfient; and they who would protract it often fall into an uneafy ftate of mind, to which darknefs, defertion, and other mournful names are given. If you would efcape from that uneafy ftate, mingle active virtue with piety, and to your prayers for others add labours of love.

THE Interceffion of JESUS, the Apoftle and High Prieft of our profeffion, is one of the many particulars in which the doctrine of mediation correfponds to human nature. He prayed for his difciples in the hour of temptation, and in the hour of forrow. It is a ftanding confolation to his friends, that " we have an advocate with " the Father, even Jefus Chrift the righ- " teous." It is a bond of union with Jefus, and a pledge of the continuance of his love. It is a new and living way by which we have boldnefs to draw near to God.

PRAYER for the Afflicted moulds the heart into a ferious frame. We think on

C   the

the worth and uncertainty of health, and view our life on earth as a pilgrimage.

BISHOP BUTLER obferves, That " com-
" paſſion is added to the general principle
" of benevolence, to give it a fpecial bias
" to the miferable, with a view to prevent
" or alleviate mifery." Agreeably to this
it may be further obferved, that thofe who
pray for others feel themfelves particularly interefted in the caufe of the afflicted,
and are difpofed to pray earneftly for them.
This may be confidered as an additional
provifion for the exercife of good offices
toward thofe who ftand moſt in need of
them.

FOR the good offices which prayer in-
fpires, a reward is provided in the prayers of thofe who receive them. It is natural for one who is deeply injured to cry
unto God againſt the oppreſſor ; and when
delivered, to pray for his deliverer. " The
" Lord requite you," is a common expreſ-
ſon of gratitude with thofe who can make
no other requital : it is one of the cafes
where

where a tendency to interceffion is felt, and the devout cherifh gratitude by pray-er for their benefactors. To the male-volent it is an alarming thought, That the cry of thofe whom he has injured is entering into the ear of the Lord ; while the humane think with pleafure, that prayers for them are rifing up as incenfe from the hearts of thofe whom they have inftructed and relieved and comforted. This pleafure is a reward fuited to the frame of devout benevolence.

EVEN when we have it not in our power to give any confiderable relief, it ftill yields fome comfort to the afflicted to fhare the fympathy of thofe around them. It is comfort to have the burden of their afflictions, the fecret workings of their fouls unfolded, and expreffed in prayer by a tender hearted Chriftian.

PRAYERS for the fick are enjoined in Scripture, and it goes with the current of the heart to offer them. When a friend is fick of an incurable difeafe, and our

friendfhip

friendfhip cannot make the cup pafs from him, we lift up our fouls in prayer to the God of all confolation. Importunity, which fome have cenfured, but which Chrift enjoins, is then felt to be a dictate of the heart as well as of the gofpel. Fervent fupplication begets a juft fenfe of fpiritual good things. As the fire of devotion burns we fet our hearts on the favour of God, and feel that happinefs depends upon it. Fervid defires toward **God** moderate every worldly defire. **Our fouls** return unto their reft. If this be the tendency of fervent prayer, the objection againft fervour is removed. If ftill it fhall be called Enthufiafm, there is nothing in a word. If an elevation of mind above this world ; if a generous love, whofe bands affliction cannot loofe ; if a fenfe of the real permanent interefts of human nature, and ardent afpirations after them——if this be enthufiafm, it is yet an enthufiafm which every good man loves to feel, in which he rejoices, yea and will rejoice.

THE

THE afflicted are difpofed in their turn
to pray for thofe who fympathife with
and minifter to them. When one is fick
unto death, thofe who are dear to him
naturally rufh into his mind, and he as
naturally commends them to God, and
commits them to his providential care. A
dying man feems nearer to God; his prayers make a deep impreffion on children and
friends; and perhaps on enemies, when he
prays God to forgive them. Eufebius tells
of a martyr who obtained an hour's re-
fpite, and employed it in prayer, fupplication, and giving of thanks for all men.
He remembered thofe who were known
and dear to him. He prayed for Chriftians, and Jews, and Gentiles; for the Em-
peror by whofe edict he fuffered, for the
executioners, and the fpectators.

THERE is an elevation and dignity in
the prayer of a dying Chriftian. His own
affliction is loft in a generous concern for
others. He was never more a citizen of
the world, and never more zealous for

the interefts of truth and virtue. Far from renouncing his attachments here, he yields his heart to all the fervour and tendernefs of love. Love was the prevailing affection of his life, and he utters his laft breath in prayers for his brethren.

THE

THE SOCIETY FOR PROPAGA-
TING CHRISTIAN KNOWLEDGE
was formed about the beginning of this
century. It has obtained countenance from
the Legiſlature, the General Aſſembly, and
many liberal Chriſtians. Much good has
been done. In the ſtate of the Highlands,
it appears that much remains to be done.
Fellow citizens in want and ignorance, have
a claim to the alms and prayers of their
happier brethren.

Some complain of the decay of piety;
and there are ſymptoms of decay. Two
occur in the printed ſtate of the Society.
One is, that twenty thouſand pounds of the
produce of the forfeited eſtates were ap-
propriated by Parliament, for erecting
ſchools in the Highlands, but never applied:
We cannot help imagining to ourſelves the
good this would have done, and regretting
that it is left undone. The other is, that
many pariſhes have no legal ſchoolmaſter:
We know not the grounds upon which the

heritors

heritors juftify themfelves ; but if it be indeed the love of money, which makes them withhold the pittance allowed by law to fchoolmafters, we muft conclude that Chriftian knowledge is of fmall moment in their eye.

THERE are other fymptoms of the decay of piety which I will not enumerate ; but, in the midft of thefe, the Society for Propagating Chriftian Knowledge is a fymptom of the firft love, and an attempt to quicken the things that are ready to die. While perfons every way eminent join in fo good a work, and the hearts of the people open, and the pleafure of the Lord profpers, we cannot think that faith and charity have failed.

THIS inftitution gives an object and an effect to Chriftian zeal. The influence of rank, and the powers of genius, and the knowledge of affairs, are exerted in the caufe of piety. Interceffion and giving of thanks accord with your pious labours. While you plant and water, you look to

God

God for the increafe : When he giveth the increafe, you offer thankfgiving.

THE exercife of devotion will enlighten your zeal, and fupport you under difcouragements, and raife you above the praife of men. To the praife of men you are juftly entitled; it is no mean reward, and it is freely given you; but, in the prefence of God, you feel and acknowledge that you have done only what was your duty to do.

You are zealous to propagate the gofpel in diftant corners; and you will be ftill more zealous where you are more immediately accountable. Command your children and your houfehold to keep the way of the Lord. Confefs Jefus before men; your example will encourage fearful and faint-hearted difciples to confefs him.

ONE end of this Inftitution is to prevent the growth of Popery. It is meet that our deliverance from that cruel fuperftition be remembered with gratitude, and that proper means be ufed for perpetuating the de-

D

liverance

liverance. One mean of acknowledged propriety and of proven fuccefs is, **to** propagate Chriftian Knowledge. A form of worfhip where the underftanding and the heart are excluded, cannot bear **the** light. Your zeal for the PROTESTANT INTEREST is becoming, while it prompts you to inftruct the ignorant.

THE fund for propagating Chriftianity is a ftanding admonition to the rich. They are impatient of the word of exhortation, and this is a filent monitor. One who has leifure and a tafte for doing good, may turn a little money to more account by beftowing it in his own way; but fome who have large eftates, and are liberally paid by the public, have not leifure to turn what they beftow to a good account : By beftowing it here that will be done. The rich are moft interefted in the public weal, and this is one way of promoting it.

SOME who are very rich are yet, from peculiar circumftances in their lot, very unhappy : From forwarding this and other good

good works, they might derive confolation.

' In the day of profperity the heart devifes
liberal things. When you fucceed to an
inheritance, or profper in trade, or obtain
a lucrative employment, or a rich alliance,
or any domeftic joy, here you may prefent
a thank-offering, and hallow your joy.

Here likewife fin-offerings may be offered. They who have deceived and cor-
rupted youth, if they be now come to a
better mind, may contribute to fortify the
young againft future deceivers.

In a commercial ftate, where money is
fo much valued, and poverty defpifed, iniquity will abound: In turning from iniquity, reftitution is effential. There are
cafes where it cannot be made to the perfons injured. The refolution of cafuifts is,
that the money fhould be given to fome
pious ufe. Here you may give it with fe-
crecy, and with confidence that it will be
properly applied.

THEY

THEY who have grown rich by traffic, without confcious fraud, have yet reafon to fufpect themfelves. The defire of gain, which is habitual to a trafficker; the opportunities for defrauding which fall in his way; the doubtful cafes which arife, and which felf-partiality is apt to determine, are grounds of fufpicion. One of a tender confcience will purify his gains by an offering.

WE cannot but obferve, even in fome of the beft characters among the rich, " one " thing wanting." They are found in the faith, and regular in their conduct, and amiable in their manners: They are not far from the kingdom of heaven. Let fuch do good, and be rich in good works; that they may lay hold on eternal life.

A LEGACY, though it be the leaft edifying and leaft meritorious charity, is better than none.

THEY who have not much to give, have an opportunity, on the return of this day, to exprefs their good wifhes by their mite.

ATTENTION

ATTENTION to this, and other good works, might correct the prefent tendency to expenfive living, by which fo many families are broken down, and credit fhaken. We may indeed tell the expenfive, how much good might be done with the price of one entertainment, or of one ornament; and they fometimes liften; for a compaffionate and expenfive turn are not incompatible. An eloquent reprefentation might draw from them confiderable fums. If I poffeffed fuch eloquence I would hefitate to exert it. It would be wrong to give to this, or any other charity, what is due to your creditors, or to thofe of your own houfe. You yourfelves would repent. The gifts of the wife, like thofe of God, are without repentance.

MODERATION in all things is a pure and permanent fource of good works. When you have tafted the pleafure of doing good, it will bear down the pleafure of expenfive fhew. Inftead of contriving additional conveniences, and ornaments, and meats, you will contrive which of them may be fpared.
Difficulty

Difficulty in paying debt arises chiefly from the purchase of superfluities. By retrenching these, you will be able to pay punctually, and have something over to indulge benevolence.

BESIDE the direct influence of this institution, it is a memorial of the importance of Christianity, and a provocation to spread it by every proper mean. Such means every Christian possesses, in some degree, by his prayers and by his pattern; by the influence of rank, and wealth, and reputation; and by his influence with those who esteem and love him. Such of us as have families may propagate Christian knowledge with success in them. Many who have families might entertain and educate one or more of the children of the poor. This appears to me a method of doing the most good at the least expence. It is rescuing a fellow creature from ignorance and bad habits. The field which we cultivate, and the plants which we rear, acquire an interest in our care: Much more the human heart, where we have sown and reared the fruits of righteousness, teoufnefs. " Whofo receiveth one of thefe " little ones in my name, receiveth me."

The number of poor children is at prefent great. The families of many foldiers and failors are left in want : Kindnefs is due to them. The portion of many orphans and fatherlefs children is loft by bankruptcy. If men who live in pleafure, and contract debt without the means of paying it, and ftoop to falfehood and fraud ; if fuch men cannot feel for the mifery they draw down on the innocent, it is the more neceffary that Chriftians endeavour to alleviate that mifery. Self-denial in this caufe, and an oeconomy which the world condemns, are facrifices with which God is well pleafed.

Other ways of doing good might be fuggefted ; but, if you be zealous for good works, your own heart will fuggeft them.

THE END,

ഗഗഗഗ

A N

INSTRUCTION

CONCERNING

O A T H S.

———— ——

Compofed for the PRESBYTERY of JEDBURGH,
in the year 1782.

ഗഗഗഗ

E

AN

INSTRUCTION

CONCERNING

OATHS.

———•—•———

THE PRESBYTERY having received information that OATHS are not duly regarded, to the unspeakable hazard of mens temporal and eternal interests, do appoint the following INSTRUCTION to be read from the pulpits in their bounds, on the day appointed for national fasting and humiliation.

THE Scripture says, That " an oath for " confirmation is the end of all strife." It is therefore lawful and right for Christians

to

to give evidence upon oath, when properly called upon to do it.

WHEN this is to be done, endeavour to compose and recollect yourselves. You pray in the morning of the day for grace to fulfil the duties, and to resist the temptations of it. Pray with particular earnestness on the morning of that day in which you are to swear, that you be not led into temptation.

IT appears from the information given, that witnesses sometimes attempt to disguise falsehood under the appearance of truth. In every part of religious and moral conduct the intention is chiefly to be regarded. If you intend when upon oath, by shifting the question and avoiding a direct answer, to conceal the truth; if you intend, by using expressions which admit of two meanings, to mislead the judge or jury; if you intend, by secret exceptions or additions, to render your assertion different from what it is understood to be; if by such ways as these, you intend to conceal or disguise

guife the truth, fo as to obftruct or pervert
the courfe of juftice, you bear falfe witnefs
and take God's name in vain. He fees
through all your difguifes. You cannot
deceive him, but you fatally deceive yourfelves.

" Wo unto you ye blind guides," faid
our Lord to the Scribes and Pharifees,
" which fay, whofo fhall fwear by the tem-
" ple it is nothing, but whofo fhall fwear
" by the gold of the temple he is a debtor.
" Ye fools and blind, for whether is great-
" er, the gold or the temple that fanctifies
" the gold?" Prevarication upon oath was
one of the deep corruptions of true religion
which Jefus came into this world to con-
demn. There was no guile found in his
mouth. Simplicity and godly fincerity are
marks of his difciples. A Chriftian is bound
to truth by higher motives than the fear of
men, nor does he hold himfelf innocent
merely becaufe human laws cannot reach
him. He fears God who fearches the heart,
and is able to deftroy both foul and body
in hell.

EVIL

EVIL muſt not be done that good may come. You muſt not ſwear falſely to procure any ſeeming good. It may ſeem excuſable to ſwerve from truth a little in your oath, for the advantage of the town or of any community to which you belong, or of any party or faction you eſpouſe: it may ſeem grateful to a rich man who favours you, to give your evidence a turn in his favour: it may ſeem generous, by a little prevarication, to ſerve the intereſts of a friend: it may ſeem an act of filial love to ſcreen your father's property from his creditors, by ſwearing that it is your's: it may ſeem compaſſionate, by bearing falſe witneſs, to ſcreen the guilty from puniſhment. " There " is a way which ſeemeth right unto a man, " but the end thereof are the ways of " death." Truth and juſtice are of higher and more indiſpenſible obligation than generoſity and affection and compaſſion.

" Thou ſhalt not reſpect the perſon of " the poor, nor honour the perſon of the " mighty : Thine eye ſhall not pity," are laws to the witneſs as well as to the judge. When

When giving evidence upon oath you are acting for the public, promoting the courfe of juftice, fulfilling the duty of a citizen. Private confiderations and paffions of every kind fhould then be facrificed to the public good. It is for the good of the Public that truth prevail and juftice be done.

CONSIDER yourfelf not as a witnefs for the party at whofe inftance you are called, fo as to fay every thing which may ferve his caufe and nothing againft it, but rather as a witnefs to the truth. Pretend not to give a full account of things you do not fully and certainly know. Do not favour a poor man in his caufe, nor honour the perfon of the mighty. Neither give your evidence a turn to the advantage of a generous man, nor to the prejudice of an oppreffor. Suffer not zeal for a good caufe, nor abhorrence of evil to tranfport you beyond the facred boundary of truth. If you perceive that the judge or jury miftake your meaning, interpofe to fet them right. If you know any material circumftance which

has

has not been afked, it is fit to mention it; and if, after mature recollection, a doubt about any fact remains, it is fit to exprefs that doubt. To tell all the truth, and nothing but truth, is what an oath requires.

A WITNESS muft begin his teftimony with avowing himfelf impartial. It is a wife precaution. Friendfhip or attachment, favours received or expected, ill-will or jealoufy or envy, eventual gain or lofs, are biaffes even with the upright. Let a man therefore examine himfelf.

WHEN perfonal interefts or paffions are involved in the oath, there is fpecial caufe for felf-examination. A man not wholly unprincipled may be led, through avarice, anger at being profecuted, and a pride in adhering to what he has often faid, to fwear falfely; and yet when the heat of conteft is over, when the diſhonourable victory is gained, and the mean prize contemplated, when the whole is reviewed in fober fadnefs; the voice of confcience is heard again,

its

its violated rights again are vindicated. He finds no reft till he gives back what he has got by perjury.

IF this be an account of what really happens, it is a warning to judges, to delay adminiftering an oath till other means of decifion be tried, and till the man who is to fwear has time to think : It is a warning to thofe who litigate, to commune with their own hearts before it be too late.

WHERE there is a ftrong temptation to fwear falfely, be in proportion watchful and jealous over yourfelves.

THEY who manufacture Excifeable Goods or deal in Foreign Articles, are particularly expofed to temptation. If any reconcile their minds to habitual perjury, becaufe the profits of trade and provifion for their families are interwoven with guilt, neceffity is laid upon us to undeceive them: We dare not heal fo dangerous a wound flightly, nor fay peace peace, where there is no peace. God muft be loved more than the world,

F   temporal

temporal muſt yield to everlaſting intereſts. The practice of falſe ſwearing muſt be renounced, the accurſed fruits of it reſtored, and a contrite heart offered to the God of mercy.

Oaths are ſometimes adminiſtered, both by civil and church courts, in caſes of Fornication and Adultery. A guilty man is tempted from ſhame and avarice to ſwear falſely. While depreſſed by the recollection of guilt, he is called to ſacrifice his reputation and worldly intereſt, by aſſuming a diſgrace and burden from which a falſe oath might redeem him; and, though temptation prevailed in an unguarded hour, he is now called upon to ſhew himſelf incapable of deliberate and deep iniquity. The ſituation is very hazardous; it is that of a man who has wandered from the right road, and is come to a paſs from whence he muſt return or loſe himſelf. Some have ſworn to their innocence, before juſtices of the peace, to avoid the maintenance of a child, who are neverthelefs ſhrewdly ſuſpected of guilt; and who endeavour to ſoothe their
conſciences

confciences with nice diftinctions about the time and manner of their guilt. Some have demanded the oath of purgation from a church court, who afterwards confeffed. Others have confeffed after they had fworn. And others, it is to be feared, have gone to God with a lie in their right hand. We exhort thofe who have been overtaken in fuch faults, as they tender the divine mercy, not to aggravate their guilt. The door of mercy is yet open, but perjury fears the confcience and quenches the fpirit of holinefs. Obferve by the way, how one fin leads to another. Unlawful pleafure may lead to perjury and poifon. " Her houfe is " the way to hell, leading down to the " chambers of death."

THERE are laws about Killing Game. Perfons accufed of breaking thefe laws are fometimes examined upon oath. They may be tempted through ignorance, or poverty, or perhaps an opinion that thefe laws are oppreffive and the penalties fevere, to fwear falfely. Obedience to the laws of the land is a duty, when they require nothing which

God

God forbids, and forbid nothing which he requires. If in any inftance they bear hard on the lower ranks; the poor to whom the gofpel is preached, muft confider it as one of the trials annexed to a low eftate, in which they are called to fuffer rather than fin. It were indeed to be wifhed, that the Legiflature would repeal laws which are confeffedly fevere ; and, in the mean time, that they who execute them would do it with mildnefs and moderation : They would thereby confult the interefts of liberty and humanity, and prevent fome poor unhappy men from endangering their eternal falvation.

OATHS are, from time to time, adminiftered about the Tax on Candles. There is reafon to apprehend, that the hurry and want of folemnity on the one hand, and on the other your forgetfulnefs and inaccuracy, and perhaps felf-deceit in paying the duty by a heavier weight than you can purchafe them by, may prove a fnare. It were pity that the confciences of Chriftians fhould be defiled, or even run a rifk of defilement for

such

fuch a trifle. It is fubmitted to the confide-
ration of tender Chriftians, whether it were
not better to purchafe candles, and endeavour to make up the profit in manufactu-
ring by thrift in ufing them.

A PRISONER who profeffes upon oath
to furrender his effects to his creditors, and
yet fecretes or referves a part, " lies not on-
" ly unto men but unto God." Poverty
may be fuftained when it is not brought on
nor accompanied by guilt. The love of
many to whom much is given is not yet
waxed cold, nor is the hand of the Almighty
fhortened. But if you retain what is not
your's, in defiance of divine and human laws,
a curfe overfhadows you.

In the late act relating to Bankrupts many oaths are required, and we muft thence
warn you againft frefh temptations to fwear
falfely.

IT IS MATTER OF LAMENTATION that
oaths abound fo exceedingly. It may be faid

of

of Britain as it was of Judah, " becaufe of
" fwearing the land mourns." Falfe fwearing is a national evil. All ranks fhould
confpire to avert it. In framing and a-
mending laws, every ftrong temptation
to it fhould be withdrawn. Oaths fhould
never be impofed nor taken when they can
be avoided, They fhould be accompanied
with a clear explanation and with due folemnity. All tendency to prevaricate fhould
be checked, and prevarication punifhed.
The partiality of Counfellors for their cli-
ents fhould be bounded by a fuperior regard to truth. Among thofe who litigate,
let no matter be pufhed unneceffarily the
length of fwearing. It is againft charity
to provoke a man of feeble virtue to for-
fwear ; his perjury defiles the land and
hardens himfelf.

WERE Lawgivers to liften, it might be
fuggefted, that reverence for oaths is leffen-
ed by their frequency ; that perplexing
oaths, annexed to offices of truft, exclude
the confcientious ; that revenue oaths give
premiums to the impious ; that there is
danger

danger in obliging men either to perjure or
betray themfelves ; that political paffions
and commercial interefts, when bounded
by oaths on every fide, and obftructed at e-
very ftep, will at laft break through them ;
that one who has made light of excife and
cuftom-houfe and election oaths, is prepared
to make light of oaths which affect private
property and life ; that a perjurer is fit for
treafon. The ftrongeft pillar may be over-
loaded, and when an oath breaks down, the
fabric of civil government will fhake.

OUR influence is chiefly with the lower
ranks, and our object is, to make them un-
derftand and fear an oath.

LET the words of an oath be pondered.

" GOD is my witnefs." It awakens the
remembrance of God, of his all-feeing eye,
of the pleafant countenance with which he
beholds the upright. You blufh to tell a
lie in the prefence of one who can detect
you, much more to fwear that you have received no bribe nor promife of good deed,

in

in the prefence of one from whom you received them. Why do you thus ftand in awe of a fellow-creature? Why are you afhamed and afraid of guilt in the prefence of a man like yourfelf? It is becaufe the image of God is ftamped upon him, and becaufe that image reflects an approbation of truth and an abhorrence of falfehood. If a human prefence operates thus powerfully, fhall not the prefence of God operate with all-powerful influence? Only admit this truth into your heart, while upon oath, that God is prefent with you, and its influence will be all-powerful. A fenfe of God's prefence corrects the errors of the underftanding and of the heart. The difference betwixt right and wrong appears. The obligation to do right is felt. There is a confcious dignity and pleafure in the divine approbation and complacence.

" So help me God." Help me to fulfil the facred obligation I now come under. So help me in the hour of folemn devotion, when thou beftoweft the blefling from on high on the man who has not fworn deceitfully.

fully. So help me at my utmost need. There are scenes of danger and of sorrow through which we have all to pafs, when the help of man is vain, when our hope is in God: To fwear falfely is to renounce that hope.

" As I fhall anfwer." Significant and awful words ! The tribunal of God rifes to my view, at which I fhall anfwer. Books are opened, which contain the actions and the thoughts of men, where the appeal I now make is recorded. The world and its tranfitory interefts difappear. My foul wait thou only upon God. Judge me, O Lord, for I have walked in mine integrity.

FEAR AN OATH. God's prefence is awful. His judgment makes us afraid. This fear, which fo well becomes us, and which all may cherifh, is a better prefervative from falfehood than profound reafoning. " The difputers of this world darken coun-
" fel. Wife men after the flefh feek deep
" to hide their counfel from the Lord, and
" to make his law of none effect." The

G   Greeks

Greeks were at the fame time a learned and a perfidious people. The moft learned order of the Roman church were the moft prefumptuous teachers of perfidy. Ingenuity is not needed for the obfervance, but for the breach of an oath. " My fon, ceafe " from the inftruction that caufeth to err. " Behold, to fear the Lord that is wifdom."

Avoid fwearing whenever it can be lawfully avoided. As much as lieth in you live peaceably with all men. Stir not up the angry fpirit of litigation for a fmall matter. If you be humble, preferring peace to money and victory, you may efcape much litigation, and the habitual fwearing of the litigious. Avoid as much as poffible thofe branches of trade and manufacture which are compaffed about with enfnaring oaths. Smuggling is a trade directly finful. " A " little that a righteous man hath, is better " than the riches of many wicked."

The fear of an oath overcomes other fears. You are called perhaps to give a report upon oath, founded on fkill in your profeffion.

profeffion. The fear of reflections from your brethren of the fame profeffion, of offending a great man whofe intereft is at ftake, and of fuffering in your future employment fubfide; for the fear of God is before your eyes. You exercife your profeffional fkill with calm ferious attention, and give a report according to truth.

THERE are forms of oaths appointed by the Legiflature in particular cafes, and he that fears an oath will confider before taking them. He will not reft indolently in the opinion and practice of another when he himfelf muft fwear. In a matter of fuch confequence he finds it prudent to fee with his own eyes, to ufe his own reafon, to liften to his own confcience, to think and judge and act for himfelf. He will avoid fwearing while a doubt remains in his own mind. Here, if any where, the fafe fide fhould be chofen. It is doubtlefs the fafe fide to avoid even a rifk of fwearing falfely. If temporal intereft muft be refigned, if the favour of the great muft be forfeited, if ambition muft be checked; they are facrifices

with

with which God is well pleafed. An approving confcience is an ample recompence.

COMPARE calmly the two ftates: Of one in place and favour and opulent circumftances, but who has made his way through falfe oaths ; and of one in humble circumftances who retains his integrity.

WHEN a promiffory oath is to be taken, it is meet to confider before hand the nature and extent of the obligation we are to come under. After vows it is too late to make enquiry.

IN fwearing allegiance to the King, we fhould attend to the duties of a fubject, and refolve to fulfil them. Let the remembrance of that oath check all tendency to faction and difloyalty ; and excite every one in his fphere to fupport a conftitution, which it is our happinefs to enjoy, as well as our duty to maintain.

WHEN an oath of fidelity in an office of truft muft be taken, let us enquire if we
have

have ability and time and a firm purpofe to fulfil the duties of it. Let thofe who have taken fuch an oath remember, that it implies not only a refolution at the time, but endeavours afterward to fulfil their duty. It is intended as a fecurity to others with whom we are connected by our office for the faithful difcharge of it ; and to ourfelves it ought to be a conftant remembrancer to avoid careleffnefs and floth, as well as direct unfaithfulnefs.

AVOID THE SINS WHICH LEAD TO PERJURY.

THE practice of fwearing in common converfation, fo abfurd in itfelf, and fo expreffive of emptinefs, ill-manners, and an undifciplined mind, is further aggravated as it leads to perjury. One who has broke through the reftraints of decency, is prepared to break through other reftraints. He can hardly retain reverence for a name which he daily profanes, and a tribunal to which he appeals about every trifle ; nor ftand in awe of damnation, which he lightly im-

imprecates on the fouls of others and on his own foul.

Some have a practice, in their private tranfactions, of ufing the form and words of an oath. In making bargains, for example, they ufe the facred name, and aver fuch and fuch particulars concerning their goods to be true, as they fhall anfwer. In juftifying themfelves they call God to witnefs. In borrowing money, they wifh, if they do not pay at the appointed time, that they may never fee his face in mercy. The communication of Chriftians upon fuch occafions fhould be " yea yea, nay nay; for " whatfoever is more than thefe cometh of " evil." If folemn affeverations be ufed to cloak falfehood, it is guilt highly aggravated.

An habitual regard for truth is a mean of avoiding perjury. Religious and moral obligations corroborate each other. One who is afraid to tell a lie, thinks of fwearing to it with horror : But the band of religion is feeble when the band of truth is loofed.

loofed. One who is accuftomed to difguife
or conceal truth, and to fhape his evafive
anfwers according to humour or fear or ma-
lice, is apt to do the fame things when examined upon oath. A deliberate lie is the
ftep next to perjury. One who is cautious
in making promifes, and fcrupulous to fulfil them, will be more fo when bound by an
oath. " He changeth not, though he fwear
" to his hurt."

SOBER induftry is a mean of avoiding
temptation. Want, when it is the effect of
idlenefs mifmanagement or diffipation, may
tempt men to fwear falfely. A controverfy
about debt may be referred to your oath,
there is often no other method of deciding
it: Then the profane prodigal is prompted
by his wants to perjure himfelf. If there be
wretches who fell themfelves to commit
this great tranfgreffion, they are probably
fuch as have contracted habits of floth and
luxury without means of gratifying them.

LET witneffes beware of thofe who would
tamper with them. They court and flatter;
they

they intimate advantages if you can truly
fwear fo and fo; they hint whom it will o-
blige, and what power he has to do you
good or ill; they endeavour to talk you into
a perfuafion that you know or remember
as they would have you.——Thefe are the
children of the wicked one, they are doing
his work, plotting your eternal ruin. Stop
your ear againft their infinuations, partake
not of their drink or their dainties, have no
communication with them.

We know well that they who tempt o-
thers to fwear falfely are beyond the reach
of any of the means of grace committed unto us. It is our duty however to teftify,
that thofe who employ their wealth to cor-
rupt, or their power to intimidate, or their
talents to explain away the obvious meaning of an oath; who perfuade the poor,
the fearful, or the ignorant to take God's
name in vain; that they are partakers of
the guilt in which they involve the perjurer.

PERJURY is forbidden in the firft table
of the law. It is taking God's name in
vain,

vain, which he will not hold guiltlefs. " As
" I live, faith the Lord, furely mine oath,
" which he hath defpifed, even it will I re-
" compence on his own head. The curfe
" of God fhall enter into the houfe of him
" that fweareth falfely, it fhall remain in
" his houfe, and fhall confume it, the tim-
" ber thereof and the ftones thereof." It is
an obfervation of your own, and become
proverbial among you, that one who fwears
falfely has never afterwards a day to do
well. He has hardened himfelf againft God
and he cannot profper. His mind is like the
troubled fea. In the hour of filence, and in
the hour of danger, he is haunted with this
joylefs and difmaying thought, that God is
his enemy.

FALSE WITNESS is likewife forbidden in
the fecond table of the law. It violates the
moft important human rights—property,
reputation, life. Afk the man who has fuffered by perjury, and he will tell you what a
heinous crime it is, and what deep refent-
ment it awakens. Put yourfelf in the fitua-
tion of fuch a man, and liften to the language of your own heart.

H   " IF

" If a falfe witnefs. rife up againft any " man," fays the law of Mofes, " and tefti- " fy againft him that which is wrong, then " fhall ye do unto him as he thought to have " done to his brother." If an innocent man has fuffered death through perjury, it is juft that the falfe witnefs die. " He has affaffi- " nated his brother, and contaminated with " blood the faered ftream of juftice."

By our own law, imprifonment, confifca- tion, and infamy are denounced. One who breaks down the fence by which liberty and property are fecured, forfeits his own : The violator of truth is configned to infamy. Let not the glare of wealth, nor the gloffes of cafuiftry, nor fafhionable maxims of po- litenefs efface the brand of infamy from the perjurer.

Among all nations an oath is refpected. Even the worfhippers of falfe gods are afraid to fwear falfely. It feems one of the origi- nal notices given to men, that there is an in- vifible witnefs of human actions, and a day of juft retribution. It is given to fupply the imperfection of human laws, and to ftrength- en, en, with the band of religion, every móral tie. Were it not for the facredneſs of an. oath, innocence would ceaſe to be a protection, induſtry would be vain, a good name would be a precarious treaſure, mutual confidence would ceaſe, the bands of fociety would be broken.

WHETHER we view the laws of God or of men againſt ſwearing falfely, its effects on fociety, or on the man who commits it, it appears furrounded with guilt and danger. " It is a word compaſſed about with death. " God grant it be not found in the dwell- " ings of Jacob."

THIS WARNING the Preſbytery give you from a ſenſe of duty, and a concern for your beſt intereſts, whether you will hear or whether you will forbear. If you lend a deaf ear, and harden yourſelves in ſin, it ſhall yet be known that the fervants of the Lord have been among you, that the trumpet has not given an uncertain found, that ye have not periſhed for lack of knowledge. Your blood ſhall not be required at their hands.

WE

WE hope better things of you. It is our joint and fervent prayer, that the mean now ufed may prove effectual. We are ready to give you further inftruction, both in public and private, on this and every other branch of religious and moral conduct. If ever you be at a lofs to difcern fin and duty, and to apply the law of God to your own cafe, we are ready to give our advice, when you are pleafed to afk it, with the affection of a father and the faithfulnefs of a friend.

IF you take this admonition in good part, and if the fruits of it fhall appear; if you difcover a tendernefs of confcience, and an habitual regard to the divine law; and if, in difficult and trying fteps, you be chiefly folicitous to approve yourfelves unto God; it will be a ground of hope, that thofe days of fafting and humiliation, which have fo often returned, will at laft be changed into a day of thankfgiving; that righteoufnefs and peace will meet together in our land, filling our hearts with gladnefs and our mouths with praife.

THE END.